The Scottish Kitchen

First published in 2007 by

The Appletree Press Ltd
The Old Potato Station
14 Howard Street South
Belfast BT7 1AP

Tel: +44 (028) 90 24 30 74
Fax: +44 (028) 90 24 67 56
Email: reception@appletree.ie
Web: www.appletree.ie

Copyright © Appletree Press, 2007
Text by Paul Harris and Marion Maxwell
Photographs © As acknowledged on page 93

A catalogue record for this book is available from the British Library.

The Scottish Kitchen

ISBN: 978 1 84758 007 8

Desk and Marketing Editor: Jean Brown
Copy-editing: Jim Black and Laura Armstrong
Picture Research: Laura Armstrong
Designer: Stuart Wilkinson
Production Manager: Paul McAvoy

9 8 7 6 5 4 3 2 1

AP3414

The Scottish Kitchen

Paul Harris and Marion Maxwell

Contents

Introduction

This is by no means any sort of attempt at a complete survey of Scottish cuisine: other writers have attempted this at greater length and in more substantial volumes and for readers whose appetite is further stimulated we have included a list of recommended reading. Rather, this is a collection of some favourite traditional Scottish dishes which are typical of the cuisine of Scotland.

Scotland is a vast larder with fish, fowl and game a-plenty and many of these recipes reflect the availability of venison, pheasant, grouse, salmon and other foods which may, by some people, be regarded as luxury foods. But this is balanced out by traditional recipes for soups, fish and meat dishes enjoyed by the fisher folk and crofters of Scotland for generations. Read and enjoy.

The variety and richness of Scottish baking is also looked at: the homely bannocks, scones and oatcakes; the sophisticated confections turned out by the ancient Incorporation of Baxters in Edinburgh; the oatmeal gingerbread of the Orkneys; and the delicious breads and cakes served in Glasgow tea-rooms in the nineteenth century. Long after the arrival of the baker's cart, a love of home baking still flourishes. Here, then, are ideas aplenty if you are wanting a wee something to have with your flycup!

A note on measures

In Scotland, as in the rest of Britain, Imperial measures – pounds, pints, etc. – are most widely used although the dreaded metric measures – kilogrammes, litres, etc. – are now making incursions thanks to the efforts of the EU and our European neighbours. Both types of measure are given in the recipes here. Stick to one though – do not mix the two measures in any one recipe or culinary disaster is likely to result.

All recipes, unless otherwise stated, are for four people of normal appetite.

BREAKFAST
DISHES

Porridge

'Oats: a grain, which in England is generally given to horses...
in Scotland supports the people.'

Dr Johnson

Few would argue with Robbie Burns that porridge is 'Chief o'
Scotia's food'. There are two important things to remember:
always refer to porridge in the plural as 'them' and eat them
standing up. Also soak overnight for best results.

600ml/1pt water
1 level tsp salt
50g/2oz oatmeal

Boil water, add salt, sprinkle in oatmeal, stirring. Boil and
place lid on pan. Simmer for 30-40 minutes, stirring frequently.
If coarse oatmeal is used allow extra cooking time.
    Soak overnight to reduce cooking time.

Herrings in Oatmeal

The staple diet of many Scots for centuries, the herring is a popular breakfast dish. Split before curing they are known as kippers.

4 herrings (cleaned)
2 tsp salt
pinch of pepper
100g/4oz medium oatmeal
fat for frying

To Serve:
lemon slices
parsley

Bone the fish. Mix the salt and pepper with the oatmeal and coat each herring on both sides. Press the seasoned oatmeal mixture firmly into the fish.

Heat a little fat in the frying pan. Fry over a medium heat until lightly brown on one side, then turn over and cook the other side (approximately 3 minutes per side).

Drain the fish. Serve with a lemon slice and parsley.

Buttery Rowies

These light and flaky yeast rolls are a breakfast speciality from Aberdeen. They are best eaten fresh, spread with butter, but they freeze well and can be reheated by toasting. They are also known as Aberdeen Butteries. It is said that Aberdeen fishermen used to take them out to sea: the fat content kept them warm in the North Sea.

450g/1lb strong plain flour
pinch salt
25g/1oz fresh yeast
1 tbsp sugar or honey
425ml/15 fl oz tepid water
225g/8oz butter
110g/4oz white pastry fat

Makes 15

Sift flour and salt into a warm bowl. Cream yeast with sugar or honey and when frothy add to flour, together with enough water to make a medium soft dough. Mix well, cover with a damp cloth and set aside in a warm place for 30-45 minutes or until doubled in size. Cream butter and pastry fat together. Roll out the dough on a floured surface to form a long strip. Dot one-third of the butter mixture over the pastry, then fold in three as for flaky pastry and roll out again. Repeat this process twice using the remaining butter mixture. Roll out pastry and then cut out small rounds or ovals. Place on a greased and floured tray, cover again with a damp cloth and leave aside in a warm place to prove for another 30-45 minutes.

Preheat oven to gas mark 6, 200°C, 400°F, and place a roasting tin half-filled with boiling water on the floor of the oven to create a moist heat. Bake for 15-20 minutes, then remove the water and bake for a further 5-10 minutes until nicely golden.

Oatcakes

Made from one of our oldest native crops, *bannocks* or oatcakes were baked on a heated hearthstone or griddle and then dried out before the fire on the "banna rack".

25g/1oz plain flour
pinch salt
pinch baking soda
110g/4oz medium oatmeal
25g/1oz butter, margarine or bacon fat
¼ cup boiling water

Makes 4

Sift the flour, salt and baking soda into the oatmeal. Melt the butter, margarine or fat in boiling water and add to the dry ingredients. Mix until the mixture is a spongy mass (a little extra water can be used if necessary).Turn mixture on to a surface covered with plenty of dry oatmeal and scatter more on top. Flatten the dough and roll out until ½ cm/¼ inch in thickness, then place a dinner plate on top and trim into a neat circle. Scatter on more oatmeal and rub it in all over the surface. Cut into quarters before baking on either a griddle or in the oven.

Griddle method: Place the oatcakes on a heated griddle or heavy pan over medium heat and bake until they dry out and curl. Then place under a grill at medium heat to cook the top of the oatcakes.

Oven method: Bake at gas mark 4, 180ºC, 350ºF for 20-30 minutes or until dried out.

Arbroath Smokies

These are small haddock, cleaned but not split open, salted, tied in pairs by the tails and then hung on wooden spits above a fire – preferably of oak or silver birch chips.

4 whole smoked haddock
450ml/¾pt milk
salt and pepper
butter

Separate the pairs of Arbroath smokies and lay them in a shallow dish.

Pour on the milk and add salt and pepper. Spread on butter and cover with foil.

Cook in a moderate oven (gas mark 4, 180°C, 350°F) for 25-30 minutes.

Tattie Scones

Made from leftover potatoes, these are delicious eaten straight from the frying pan spread with plenty of butter and sometimes with sugar, syrup or honey. They are also popular fried with a cooked breakfast.

225g/8oz warm cooked potato
½ tsp salt
25g/1oz butter, melted
50g/2oz plain flour

Makes 8

Mash potatoes well. Add salt and butter, then work in enough flour to make a pliable dough. Divide the dough in two and roll out on a floured surface to form two circles 22 cm/9 inch in diameter and ½ cm/¼ inch in thickness.

Cut each circle into quarters and bake on a hot griddle or pan for about 5 minutes or until browned on both sides. Some people like to grease the baking surface, while others prefer a light dusting of flour for a drier effect.

STARTERS AND SOUPS

Cock-a-Leekie

This is probably Scotland's most famous soup and is often found on the menu at a Burns Supper or St Andrew's Night dinner. From the humblest crofts to the grandest of royal palaces this was an established favourite. Here is the special recipe of Rosa Mattravers, cook to Theodora, Lady Forbes, on Donside in Aberdeenshire.

1 boiling fowl
3 rashers lean bacon (chopped)
large veal or beef marrow bone (optional)
parsley, thyme and a bay leaf
12 leeks (chopped)
water to cover
salt and pepper
100g/4oz cooked prunes

Place chicken, chopped bacon, marrow bone, herbs and most of the leeks into a large saucepan and cover with water. Put the lid on it and let it simmer for 2-3 hours, topping up with more water if necessary, until the bird is cooked.

Season to taste, then strain, picking out the chicken and cutting it into serving pieces and spooning out the marrow from the bone. Add these to the soup, together with the stoned prunes, and the remaining chopped leeks. Simmer gently for 10-15 minutes.

Partan Bree

'Partan' is the Scots word for crab and 'bree' means a liquid. This soup was traditionally a firm favourite with Scots fisherfolk.

175g/6oz rice
600ml/1pt milk
1 large boiled crab
600ml/1pt white stock
dash/8 drops anchovy essence
dash/8 drops tabasco
salt and pepper
mace
450ml/¾pt thin cream
cayenne pepper to taste

Boil the rice in the milk until it becomes soft. Take the meat out of the crab and put it to one side. Sieve the rice, milk and soft crab meat. Stir in the stock, anchovy essence, tabasco and seasoning to taste.

Bring gently to the boil and add a pinch of mace and the cream. Garnish with flaked claw meat and cayenne pepper.

Cullen Skink

This is not an offensive small animal but a traditional recipe for soup from the Moray Firth area. 'Skink' comes from the Gaelic and means 'essence'.

1 large smoked or finnan haddock
cold water to cover
1 chopped onion
900ml/1½ pints milk
mashed potatoes as needed
15g/½oz butter
salt and pepper
mace
2 tbsp cream
parsley

Skin the haddock and put into a shallow pan or casserole dish, and add just enough cold water to cover. Bring slowly to the boil. Simmer until the consistency of the haddock becomes creamy.

Remove from the pan and part the flesh from the bones. Break the fish into flakes. Return the bones to the water in the pan and add the onion. Cover and simmer gently for 20 minutes. Strain this stock.

Return stock to a clean pan and bring to the boil. In another pan bring the milk to the boil and add to the stock with the flaked fish.

Simmer for three or four minutes but do not allow to stick to pan. Stir in hot mashed potatoes to make a creamy consistency. Add butter gradually and salt, pepper and mace to taste. Stir in the cream and, before serving, scatter the chopped parsley over the hot soup. Best served with finely sliced, dry toast.

Scotch Broth

Also known as barley broth, Boswell records that Dr Johnson was particularly rude about this nourishing soup:

'...you never ate it before?'
'No sir,' replied Johnson, 'but I don't care how soon I eat it again.'

(*Journal of a Tour to the Hebrides*, 1786)

450g/1lb neck of mutton (flank or shank), alternatively flank or hough of beef
1.2l/2pt cold water
25g/1oz barley
salt and pepper
1 medium turnip (diced)
35g/1½oz shelled peas
1 leek (sliced)
1 carrot (grated)
small piece of cabbage (grated)
1 tsp minced parsley

Put meat into a large pan with enough cold water to cover. Add salt and the well-washed barley. Bring to boiling point and skim. Add salt and pepper, diced turnip, peas and leek. Simmer for one and a half hours. Half an hour before serving add the grated carrot and the cabbage.

When ready lift out the meat and cut into dice and return the flesh to the pan. Add the parsley and serve hot. Feel free to vary the vegetables according to whatever is in season.

Potted Hough

This is a tasty savoury dish, or you may prefer it as a starter.
Potting is an ancient method of preserving food.

450g/1lb hough (shin of beef)
900g/2lb beef shin bone
water to cover
1 tsp salt
6 allspice berries
6 peppercorns
1 small bay leaf
1 pinch paprika

Put the meat and bone into a pan and cover with cold water.
Bring to the boil, and simmer for about 3 hours.

Cut the meat into small pieces. Remove meat from the
bone. Return the bone to the pan, add salt, allspice berries,
peppercorns, bay leaf and paprika and boil the liquid rapidly
until it has reduced by about half. Put the meat into a large
mould, pour in the stock and put in the fridge to set. Serve
next day out of the mould, with a salad if desired.

FISH DISHES

Skye Prawns

The Skye prawn is otherwise known as a Dublin Bay prawn or langoustine. Although the following is not a traditional recipe this delicious sharp-tasting sauce provides the perfect accompaniment for the prawns.

150ml/¼pt mayonnaise
2 tsp tomato puree
pinch of paprika
dash tabasco
pepper
450g/1lb king prawns
1 tbsp double cream
1 lemon

Mix together mayonnaise, tomato puree, paprika and tabasco. Season to taste. Boil prawns in salted water for 2 minutes only. Remove and shell. Fold cream into sauce mixture and serve with prawns. Garnish with wedges of lemon and whole (unshelled) prawns.

West Coast Mussels

Mussels from the sea lochs of the west coast are delicious. To prepare them, scrub clean and boil in water. Discard any of the shells which do not open. Highland hostess The Lady Glentruim serves these *par excellence* at Glentruim Castle in Inverness.

50g/2oz breadcrumbs
100g/4oz butter
1 small onion
½ clove garlic
450g/1lb cooked mussels
salt and pepper
4 tbsp white wine

Fry breadcrumbs in half the butter and put to one side, then fry the chopped onion and garlic in the remaining butter. Put the mussels, onion, garlic and seasoning in a shallow dish and cover with wine and breadcrumbs. Heat in oven pre-set at gas mark 5, 190°C, 375°F for 10-15 minutes and serve piping hot.

Salmon Steaks

This king of fish requires very little in the way of addition or garnishing. Here is a simple recipe.

4 slices salmon (about 2 cm/¾ inch thick)
2 tbsp melted butter
salt and pepper
parsley
lemon, sliced

Wipe the salmon slices with a damp cloth and brush over with melted butter. Season with salt and pepper on both sides

Place the slices under a hot grill. Grill each side for 5 minutes or so, as necessary. Serve garnished with parsley and sliced lemon.

Parsley Sauce

This simple Parsley Sauce is an ideal accompaniment to fish.

25g/1oz butter
25g/1oz plain flour
575mls/1pint milk
seasoning
1 tbsp finely chopped parsley

Melt the butter; add the flour and stir with a wooden spoon over a gentle heat for around a minute. Slowly add the milk, then bring to the boil and season to taste, stirring continuously.

Add the finely chopped parsley and simmer gently for 5 minutes. Pour into a sauceboat and serve hot.

MAIN COURSE
DISHES

Forfar Bridies

The individual steak pies from Forfar, Angus, were immortalised by J.M. Barrie in *Sentimental Tommy*. They are the Scottish equivalent to the Cornish pasty.

Pastry
450g/1lb plain flour
pinch of salt
100g/4oz margarine
100g/4oz lard

Filling
450g/1lb chuck steak
75g/3oz prepared shredded suet
1 onion (finely chopped)
salt and pepper

Sift the flour and salt together, add the margarine and lard cut into pieces and rub in. Stir in enough cold water to make a stiff dough then turn it onto a floured surface; knead gently. Divide dough into four. Trim the steak, removing any excess fat, then pound it. Cut the meat into thin strips and mix it with the suet and onion and plenty of seasoning. Roll each piece of dough out to a 15 cm/ 6 inch round shape. Divide the filling among each and seal the edges well with water.

Make a hole in the centre of each bridie with a skewer and bake at gas mark 6, 200°C, 400°F for 20 minutes. Reduce the temperature to gas mark 4, 180°C, 350°F and bake for a further 35-45 minutes or until golden brown.

Serve hot with peas and potatoes.

Scots Mince

This wholesome Scottish family dish is sometimes known as 'Scotch Collops', from the French *escalope*, meaning thin slivers of meat. It is one of Scotland's most popular dishes to this day.

15g/½oz dripping
1 medium onion (peeled and sliced)
450g/1lb best minced beef (firmly packed)
salt and pepper
300ml/½pt beef stock
1 level tbsp oatmeal
2 bay leaves

Melt the dripping in a pan, add the onion and fry it for a few minutes. Stir in the mince and brown it carefully, stirring constantly to avoid lumps. Mix in the salt, pepper and stock together with the oatmeal and bay leaves.

Simmer for about 45 minutes or until the meat is cooked. Serve with mashed potatoes. Turnips ('neeps') are an optional extra vegetable.

Haggis

Everybody knows that a haggis is a small, scruffy, hairy animal accustomed to running through hedges backwards. It is so elusive that you will have to make do with this recipe for what many would regard as Scotland's very own national dish, always served on Burns Night.

1 sheep's paunch (stomach bag)
heart, liver and lung of sheep
1 tsp salt
black pepper, freshly ground
mace
nutmeg
2 onions (chopped)
450g/1lb beef suet
175g/6oz toasted oatmeal
450ml/¾pt stock

The following recipe is not for the weak of constitution! Wash the paunch well in cold water. Turn it inside out and scrape with a knife. Boil the heart, liver and lung until tender, hanging the windpipe out over the edge of the pan so that it drains into a bowl.

Chop the meat finely and grate the liver. Spread this out and add salt, pepper, mace, nutmeg, onions, suet and oatmeal. Mix well with stock and fill the paunch with the mixture. Leave some room for the oatmeal to swell in the cooking. Sew it up with a trussing needle and coarse thread or very fine string.

Prick all over with a needle and put into boiling water for 3 hours. Remove from the pan and place on a hotplate. Remove the threads, slit open the bag and serve steaming hot with mashed potatoes and mashed turnips ('chappit tatties' and 'bashed neeps'). Ensure suitable musical accompaniment is available (i.e. a kilted piper) before serving!

Bashed Neeps

This recipe works equally well with either turnip or swede and is the classic accompaniment to Haggis.

1 turnip or swede
50g/2oz butter
salt and pepper
pince of mace (optional)

Peel and dice the turnip then cook in boiling water for 25-30 minutes or until tender. Drain and mash well.

Add the butter and season to taste. Mix until the butter has melted throughly and serve hot.

Stovies

Simple but surprisingly delicious. The potatoes should be unblemished and of equal size. The name 'stovies' comes from the French *étouffer*, to stew in a closed vessel.

15g/½oz butter
1 large onion
2 thin slices bacon (chopped)
450g/1lb potatoes
salt and pepper
300ml/½pt hot water

Melt the butter in a pan. Peel and slice the onion and fry in the butter with the bacon. Peel and slice the potatoes and add them to the pan. Season and add the water to a depth of ½ inch.

Put the lid on the pan and cook slowly for 1-1½ hours. Stir as necessary to prevent the potatoes sticking to the pan.

Scotch Woodcock

An easily made, mouth-watering, savoury dish.

15g/½oz butter
1 egg
1 tbsp milk
salt and pepper
pinch of paprika
dash of tabasco sauce
thinly sliced toast
anchovy fillets
capers

Melt the butter, beat the egg, add milk and seasoning and scramble. Butter the toast, mound scrambled egg on top.

Place an anchovy fillet across the egg and put a caper on either side.

GAME

Roast Venison

Some of the finest venison in the world is to be found in Scotland where the deer roam free on the high mountain tops. This recipe is for roasting a large joint for serving with a traditional sauce.

1 haunch of venison (about 2.5kg/6lb)
butter
paste of flour and water
salt and black pepper
flour
2 tbsp melted butter
1 glass claret

The venison should be well hung before cooking. Sponge it with warm water and rub over with butter. Cover with greaseproof paper and over this lay a paste of flour and water so that the surface is well covered. Wrap in foil and roast for around four hours at gas mark 3, 160°C, 325°F.

Remove foil and paper and test with fork. Season with salt and black pepper, dredge with flour, baste well with melted butter and claret and brown quickly. Serve with the hot sauce.

Serving Sauce for Venison

This tasty rich sauce contrasts beautifully with the lean venison meat. Remember – venison should always be accompanied by a good Burgundy.

kidneys from venison
1 tbsp butter
1 glass port wine
1 tbsp flour
salt and pepper
1 tbsp redcurrant jelly

To make the sauce, lightly fry the venison kidneys in butter, remove them from the pan and add the port and seasoning to the pan juices.

Reduce and thicken with flour as necessary. Add the redcurrant jelly and boil. Serve over the venison.

Roast Pheasant

The hen is generally tastier than the better-looking cock. The bird should be well hung: the traditional test was to hang by the tail and when the body fell to the cellar floor it was ready for the pot!

1 pheasant
small piece of butter
redcurrant jelly
1 orange
slices of fat bacon
300ml/½pt cold water
1 small glass claret
salt and pepper

Pluck and gut the pheasant (you'll need to look elsewhere for your instructions if tackling this for the first time!); put a piece of butter, some redcurrant jelly and an orange inside the body to keep it moist. Put slices of bacon on the breasts and place the pheasant on a rack over a tray in the oven.

Cook in a moderate oven for 45-60 minutes. Just before the bird is ready, baste it with the liquid in the tray. Return to the oven, set at gas mark 7, 220°C, 435°F, and leave until brown, about 10 minutes.

Place bird on serving dish. Strain fat from tray, leaving sediment. Add 300ml/½pt cold water, skim off solidified fat; stir well, boil up on hot plate with claret and season. Serve with gravy, bread sauce and cranberry sauce or claret jelly.

Pigeon Casserole

In days of yore dovecotes were plentiful in town and country and pigeons were much favoured as a useful extra source of meat. They are cheap and distinctively flavoursome and, cooked long and slow, are excellent as a casserole dish.

2 old pigeons
100g/4oz streaky bacon
25g/1oz butter
300ml/½pt claret
150ml/¼pt water or stock
200g/8oz chopped mushrooms
2 bay leaves
salt and pepper
1 tbsp browned flour

Pluck and gut the birds. Wipe pigeons inside and out with a damp cloth. Chop bacon and fry in a shallow saucepan with a little butter. Add the pigeons and fry lightly for 5 minutes. Transfer contents of pan to a casserole dish.

Pour claret and stock into a pan. Add mushrooms, bay leaves and salt and pepper. Bring to the boil and reduce and thicken with the flour as necessary. Pour over the pigeons. Cover and cook in a slow oven, gas mark 5, 190°C, 375°F, until tender (1½-2 hours).

Grouse and Steak Pudding

Alas, now almost in the category of an endangered species, the Glorious Twelfth (of August) is no longer quite so glorious. The Red Scotch Grouse is reckoned by the *cognoscenti* to be the finest game bird in the world and now exists only in Scotland and some parts of the north of England. Hang for at least a week and roast the young birds; the older ones will make an excellent pudding.

1 old grouse
celery
1 carrot
3-4 bay leaves
½ tsp thyme
1 clove
salt and pepper
½ tbsp powdered gelatine
250g/8oz chuck steak
1 small onion
chopped parsley
shortcrust pastry
egg yolk

Bone the grouse. Make a stock with the bones, the vegetables, herbs and seasoning. Simmer for 3 hours. Add the gelatine and let cool. Slice the flesh off the grouse and cut up the meat. Season to taste.

Take a pie dish and put a layer of steak, then a layer of grouse, then a layer of onion and parsley. Finish with another layer of steak. Add half the stock and allow it to set.

Cover with pie dough, brush with egg yolk and cook for 3 hours: the oven should be hot to start with and when the pastry browns cover pie with greaseproof paper and reduce to medium oven. When cooked, add the balance of the stock through a hole in the top of the pie. Serve cold.

BREADS, SCONES AND PANCAKES

Baps

The bap is the traditional morning roll of Scotland, eaten soft, floury and warm from the oven. In the sixteenth century, a "bawbee bap" was one that sold for a halfpenny. Writing in 1955, author Victor MacClure recalls "having it stuffed with Ayrshire bacon and a fried egg to eat while hastening to beat the bell for morning school."

450g/1lb plain flour, warmed
1 tsp salt
50g/2oz lard
25g/1oz fresh yeast
1 tsp sugar
275ml/10 fl oz tepid milk and water mixed

Makes 8

Sift flour and salt into a warmed bowl. Lightly rub in lard. Cream yeast with sugar and mix with most of liquid. Mix into flour, adding remaining liquid as necessary, and knead lightly to form a soft dough. Cover with a damp cloth and leave in a warm place to rise for 1-1½ hours. Turn out on to a floured surface, knead lightly again, then form into oval shapes about 11 cm by 7.5 cm/4½ inch by 3 inch. Set well apart on a floured baking sheet then cover and set aside for 15 minutes. Preheat oven to gas mark 7, 220°C, 425°F. Brush baps with milk and sprinkle with flour. Press your finger into each bap (to prevent it blistering when cooking) and bake for 15-20 minutes. Dust with a little flour if liked.

Wheaten Bannock

Before white flour became widely available and before the advent of the baker's cart, this bread would have been a mainstay of the daily diet, the buttermilk giving it added sustenance. This up-to-date version with its healthful additions couldn't be simpler to make.

110g/4oz plain white flour
3 tsp (level) baking soda
½ to ¾ tsp salt
275g/10oz coarse wholemeal flour
275g/10oz fine wholemeal flour
80g/3oz pinhead or rolled oats
2 tbsp wheatgerm
2 tbsp bran
1 tbsp (scant) brown sugar
50g/2oz butter or margarine (or 2-2½ tbsp olive oil)
825ml/1½ pt buttermilk

Makes 2

Preheat oven to gas mark 6, 200°C, 400°F, and grease and flour two 900g/2lb loaf tins. Sieve plain flour with baking soda and salt. Stir in other dry ingredients and rub in butter or margarine (or stir in olive oil.) Gradually add the buttermilk until the mixture is slack enough to spoon into the tins.

Place in the oven and bake for 50-60 minutes. To test if the wheaten is cooked through, tap on the bottom: if it sounds hollow it is ready. Cover with a cloth until cold. This bread freezes well.

Barley Bannocks

Leeze me on thee, John Barleycorn,
Thou king o' grain!
On thee auld Scotland chaws her cood
In souple scones, the wale o' food.

Thus Robert Burns pays tribute to the fact that barley was, along with oats, the staple grain of Scotland in ancient times. This recipe is the kind of bread that was made daily on the girdle or, more primitively, on a heated hearthstone. Tradition has it that kneading should be done "sunwise", with a right-handed turn.

450g/1lb barley meal
110g/4oz plain flour
2 tsp cream of tartar
1 tsp salt
2 tsp baking soda
550ml/1 pint buttermilk

Makes 4

Sieve barley meal and flour together with cream of tartar and salt. Stir soda into buttermilk and when it fizzes, pour it into the flour mixture. Mix to a soft dough, using a little extra flour if necessary. Turn out on to a floured surface and roll out lightly until 3 cm/1½ inch thick.

Cut into rounds or divide into farls. Set on a hot girdle or electric pan and bake until underside is brown. Turn and brown on other side.

Selkirk Bannock

This round, yeasted fruit loaf was made famous in Scotland in the mid-nineteenth century by Robbie Douglas in his bakery in Selkirk Market Place. Reputedly, it was the only thing that Queen Victoria ate when she visited Sir Walter Scott's grand-daughter at Abbotsford in 1869.

110g/4oz butter
110g/4oz lard
275ml/10 fl oz milk, warmed
25g/1oz fresh yeast
½ tsp sugar
900g/2lb strong plain flour
¼ tsp salt
450g/1lb sultanas
110g/4oz chopped peel
225g/8oz caster sugar
1 tbsp each warm milk and sugar mixed to glaze

Warm all the ingredients and utensils. Soften the butter and lard, then stir in the warmed milk. Cream yeast with the sugar and add to mixture. Sift flour and salt, pour in the liquid and form a dough. Knead on a floured surface for 10 minutes, then return to the bowl. Enclose in a polythene bag and leave in a warm place for about 1 hour or until doubled in size.

Knead until smooth, add sultanas, peel and caster sugar and knead again for about 5 minutes. Shape into a flat round approximately 23 cm/9 inch in diameter and place on a greased baking sheet. Cover again and set in a warm place for 35-40 minutes.

Bake at gas mark 5, 190°C, 350°F for 60-75 minutes. A little before the end of baking time, glaze the bannock. When cooked, the bannock will sound hollow when tapped on the bottom.

Whisky Tea Brack

Tea brack derives its moisture and flavour from the strong, sweet tea in which the fruit is soaked overnight. This is my version of a recipe given to the late Theodora Fitzgibbon by her grandmother who soaked the fruit in a mixture of half tea and half whisky!

225g/8oz sultanas
225g/8oz raisins
225g/8oz soft brown sugar
½ tsp cinnamon
¼ tsp grated nutmeg
2 tbsp whisky
275ml/10 fl oz strong tea
450g/1lb self-raising flour
2 eggs, beaten
marmalade or honey to glaze
demerara sugar to dust

Place the sultanas, raisins, sugar, cinnamon, nutmeg, whisky and tea in a large bowl and soak overnight. Preheat oven to gas mark 3, 160°C, 325°F and grease and line a 20 cm/8 inch round cake tin. Stir in the sieved flour and eggs and mix well.

Bake for approximately 1½ hours. Towards end of baking time, brush with marmalade or honey and sprinkle with demerara sugar. To test if the brack is cooked insert a skewer into the centre: if it comes out clean then the brack is ready. When cold, slice and butter generously.

Buttermilk Scones

Morning coffee and afternoon tea would not be complete without fresh scones and there are so many delicious varieties. The secret of making good scones is a quick, light hand when mixing and a hot oven.

225g/8oz self-raising soda bread flour
pinch salt
25g/1oz butter or hard margarine
1 egg, beaten
140ml/5 fl oz buttermilk
egg or milk to glaze (optional)

Makes 8

Preheat oven to gas mark 8, 230°C, 450°F. Sift flour with salt and rub in butter or margarine. Make a well in the centre and pour in the egg and most of the buttermilk. Mix quickly to form a soft dough, adding a little extra buttermilk if necessary

Turn out on to a floured surface and roll out lightly until 2.5 cm/1 inch in thickness. Working quickly, cut into 5 cm/2 inch rounds. Glaze with egg or milk and set on a floured baking sheet. Bake for 15-20 minutes until light brown.

Savoury Cheese and Herb Scones

225g/8oz self-raising soda bread flour
pinch salt
25g/1oz butter or hard margarine
1 tsp dry mustard
50g/2oz grated cheese
2 tbsp fresh, chopped herbs
1 egg, beaten
140ml/5 fl oz buttermilk
egg or milk to glaze (optional)
extra grated cheese (optional)

Makes 8

Preheat oven to gas mark 8, 230°C, 450°F. Sift flour with salt and rub in butter or margarine. Add dry mustard, grated cheese and herbs to the dry ingredients.

Make a well in the centre and pour in the egg and most of the buttermilk. Mix quickly to form a soft dough, adding a little extra buttermilk if necessary.

Turn out on to a floured surface and roll out lightly until 2.5 cm/1 inch in thickness. Working quickly, cut into 5 cm/2 inch rounds. Glaze with egg or milk and if wished scatter a little grated cheese on the top of each scone. Set on a floured baking sheet. Bake for 15-20 minutes until light brown.

Scottish Pancakes

Add these airy little pancakes to your repertoire and you'll never be lost for something hot and fresh to offer to unexpected guests. Ready in minutes, they are delicious spread with lemon curd.

110g/4oz self-raising flour
½ tsp baking powder
1 dsp sugar
1 tbsp melted butter or cooking oil
1 egg, beaten
175ml/6 fl oz milk - 4oz (only just)

Makes 10

Sift flour and baking powder into a large mixing bowl. Add the sugar and stir in the butter or oil, egg and most of the milk, and mix well. Add the remaining milk until the mixture is a thick, smooth batter able to hold its shape when dropped in little rounds on a griddle or pan.

When bubbles appear on the surface turn over and cook the other side. (It is a good idea to make a trial scone to test the temperature of the griddle.) When cooked, the pancakes should be golden brown and spongy inside.

CAKES

Seed Cake

For centuries, caraway seeds have been used to add a distinctive flavour to puddings, biscuits and cakes. A handful would often be thrown in to speckle a sweetened soda bread. This rich cake, known also as 'carvie', recalls days of gracious living in substantial country houses, when visiting ladies would be offered a slice with a glass of port.

275g/10oz flour
½ tsp baking powder
¼ tsp cinnamon
¼ tsp nutmeg
225g/8oz butter
225g/8oz caster sugar
4 eggs, beaten
3 tbsp caraway seeds

Preheat oven to gas mark 3, 160°C, 325°F, and grease and line a 20 cm/8 inch cake tin. Sift flour with baking powder, cinnamon and nutmeg. In a separate bowl, cream the butter and sugar together until pale and fluffy, then gradually mix in the eggs, adding a little flour with each addition.

Fold in the rest of the flour and mix well. Reserve a teaspoon of the caraway seeds to decorate the top of the cake and stir the rest into the mixture. Bake for approximately 1½ hours, until pale gold in colour and firm to the touch.

Dundee Cake

Dundee cake, with its distinctive topping of blanched almonds, has drawn world-wide attention to the excellence of Scotland's baking tradition. With its good keeping qualities it makes a perfect special occasion cake.

225g/8oz plain flour, sifted
1 tsp (level) baking powder
140g/5oz butter
140g/5oz caster sugar
3 large eggs, beaten
2 tbsp brandy (optional)
2 tbsp milk
340g/12oz dried mixed fruit
50g/2oz chopped candied peel
2 tbsp ground almonds
1 tsp each fresh orange and lemon zest
50g/2oz glace cherries (optional)
50g/2oz whole blanched almonds

Preheat oven to gas mark 3, 170°C, 325°F, and grease and line a 20 cm/8 inch round cake tin. Sift flour with baking powder. Cream butter and sugar together until pale and fluffy.

Beat in the eggs a little at a time, stirring in a little flour with each addition. Fold in the remaining flour, adding brandy if using and stirring in a little milk, if necessary, to achieve a soft dropping consistency.

Gently fold in dried fruit, peel, ground almonds, citrus zest and cherries, if using. Turn into tin and smooth top. Arrange almonds on top and bake for 2-2½ hours. Best matured for a few days before cutting.

Boiled Fruit Cake

With the ingredients measured out in cupfuls (a standard breakfast cup will do) and no creaming or rubbing in to be done, this cut-and-come-again cake is an established favourite.

1 cup water
225g/8oz butter
1 cup soft brown sugar
½ cup peel
1½ cups raisins
1¼ cups sultanas
¼ cup cherries
1 tsp mixed spice
2 cups flour
1 tsp baking soda
2 eggs, beaten

Put first eight ingredients into a large saucepan and bring to a boil. Simmer gently for 20 minutes, then set aside to cool. Preheat oven to gas mark 4, 180°C, 350°F, and grease and line a 20 cm/8 inch cake tin.

Sieve the flour and baking soda into the fruit mixture and add the beaten eggs. Mix well, then turn into a cake tin and bake for 1-1½ hours or until cooked through. (Reduce the temperature towards the end of the cooking time if necessary.) Cool in the tin for 15 minutes, then turn out on to a rack.

This cake will keep well if stored in an airtight tin.

Featherlight Sponge Cake

This light-as-air cake is often used as a yardstick for judging the best baker in the parish, some of whom will swear by using duck eggs for extra volume. Perfect simply sandwiched with jam and cream, this basic mixture can also be transformed into a swiss roll, a layered gateau or a trifle base.

4 large eggs, separated
4oz/110g caster sugar
4oz/110g self-raising flour, sieved

Preheat oven to gas mark 4, 180°C, 350°F, and grease and line two 18 cm/7 inch cake tins. Beat egg yolks and sugar together until very pale and thick, then set aside. In a separate bowl, beat the egg whites until they stand in stiff peaks.

Fold the egg whites into the egg and sugar mixture, then gently fold in the flour. Divide the mixture between the cake tins and bake in the middle of the oven for about 25-30 minutes, until the sponge has shrunk slightly from the sides of the tins and is firm and springy to the touch.

When cold, sandwich together with jam, cream, fresh fruit, lemon curd or a combination of these. Finish with a dusting of caster sugar, or make a pretty pattern by sprinkling icing sugar over a doily set on the cake.

Scripture Cake

This delicious fruit cake is perfect for Sunday tea and for entertaining visitors. The recipe is cleverly devised to send you thumbing through your Bible to decipher the ingredients. The results, of course, are divine!

110g/4oz Jeremiah Ch. I v. 11
340g/12oz Jeremiah Ch. XXIV v. 2
340g/12oz I Chronicles Ch. XII v. 40
500g/1lb 2oz Leviticus Ch. II v. 2
2 tsp (level) Galatians Ch. V v. 9
1 tsp (level) Solomon Ch. IV v. 14
pinch Matthew Ch. V v. 13
6 Job Ch. XXXIX v. 14
340g/12oz Isaiah Ch. VII v. 15
450g/1lb Jeremiah Ch. VI v. 20
½ cup Solomon Ch. IV v. 11
2 tbsp I Samuel Ch. XIV v. 29

Preheat oven to gas mark 3, 180°C, 350°F and grease and line a 22 cm/9 inch cake tin. Blanch, peel and chop the almonds. Chop the figs. Sift flour with baking powder, cinnamon and salt.

Cream butter and caster sugar until fluffy. Gradually mix in beaten eggs, adding a little flour with each addition. Fold in the rest of the flour along with the honey, milk and fruit. Turn into tin and bake for approximately 2¼ hours. The cake is ready when a skewer is inserted and comes out clean.

Black Bun

This rich fruit cake was traditionally eaten on Twelfth Night but in later years it became associated with Hogmanay.

Pastry:
350g/12oz plain flour
pinch salt
25g/1oz sugar
175g/6oz butter
6 tbsp iced water

Filling:
450g/1lb each currants and raisins
175g/6oz candied peel
225g/8oz almonds, chopped and blanched
225g/8oz plain flour
225g/8oz soft brown sugar
2 eggs, beaten
1 tsp each ground ginger, allspice and grated nutmeg
¼ tsp ground black pepper
1 tsp each cream of tartar and baking soda
75-150ml/3-5 fl oz whisky or brandy
milk to bind
egg yolk to glaze

First make the pastry: sift dry ingredients, rub in butter and bind to a paste using the iced water, then rest the dough in the fridge. Preheat oven to gas mark 4, 180°C, 350°F.

Grease and line a 20 cm/8 inch, round cake tin. Roll out pastry thinly and use to line the tin, keeping enough for a lid. Mix all filling ingredients in a large bowl, and add enough milk to bind. Pack in mixture and seal with the lid.

Prick lid all over with a fork and glaze with the egg. Make a steam slit and bake for 2 hours. Reduce heat to gas mark 1, 140°C, 275°F and bake for a further 1 hour until the top is golden. Cool before turning out.

Chocolate Whisky Cake

Every baker's repertoire will include a favourite recipe for chocolate cake. Lending a distinctive Scottish flavour to this one is a smooth whisky icing. There is also a surprise ingredient in the cake itself which contributes to its wonderful moist texture. See if your guests can identify what it is!

Sponge:
175g/6oz self-raising flour
½ tsp salt
50g/2oz good dark chocolate
110g/4oz butter
175g/6oz caster sugar
80g/3oz cooked mashed potato
2 eggs, beaten
4 tbsp milk

Filling:
110g/4oz good dark chocolate
125ml/4 fl oz double cream
50g/2oz icing sugar
3 tbsp whisky

Preheat oven to gas mark 5, 190°C, 375°F, and grease and line two 20 cm/8 inch cake tins. Sift flour and salt into a mixing bowl. Melt chocolate in a bowl placed over a saucepan of hot water. In a separate bowl, cream butter and sugar together until fluffy, then beat in the chocolate and mashed potato. Gradually beat in the eggs, adding a little flour with each addition.

Fold in the rest of flour and stir in the milk. Divide mixture between cake tins and bake for 25-30 minutes. Remove from oven and after a few minutes, turn out on to a cooling rack

While the cake is cooling make the filling. Melt the chocolate as before, stir in the other ingredients and mix well. Use the filling to sandwich the sponge layers together and coat the top and sides of the cake.

Sair Heidies

A testimony to the Scottish sense of humour, these "sore heads" used to be popular in Grampian bakeries. The straight-sided cakes are wrapped in paper "bandages" and have domed heads crusted with crushed lump sugar representing "aspirin"! They are traditionally baked in special rings, but you can improvise by using metal pastry cutters, or even muffin tins.

140g/5oz self-raising flour
50g/2oz margarine
50g/2oz caster sugar
2 eggs
crushed lump sugar to decorate

Makes 10

Preheat oven to gas mark 6, 200°C, 400°F. Using greaseproof paper or firm writing paper, cut out ten paper jackets, 16 cm by 4.5 cm/6½ by 2 inch. Brush both sides of the jackets with oil, then set rings on a baking tray and line with the jackets

Whisk all ingredients for buns together thoroughly and spoon into the rings. Sprinkle with crushed sugar. Bake for about 15 minutes. Leave to cool for a few minutes, then ease out of rings.

Parlies

These cakes are said to have been popular with members of the Scottish parliament. Golden syrup – itself, incidentally, the invention of a Scottish sugar firm – can be used instead of treacle. Though it's not traditional, you could ice your parlies with a dab of orange-flavoured water icing, topped with a sliver of crystallised ginger.

50g/2oz caster sugar
110g/4oz butter or margarine
225g/8oz flour
1 tsp ground ginger
1 small egg
2 tbsp treacle, warmed

Preheat oven to gas mark 4, 180°C, 350°F. Cream sugar and butter together until fluffy. Sift flour with ginger. Stir egg into treacle and add, along with the flour, to the creamed butter

Drop dessertspoonfuls of the mixture on to a greased baking sheet, leaving room for spreading. Bake for 15-20 minutes until golden. Cool on a rack.

Scottish Snowballs

A universal favourite in home bakeries, there are no prizes for guessing how these buns get their name. They bear, however, only a passing resemblance to the "snow cake", a sweet, white cake made with arrowroot and egg whites, for which Mrs. Beeton gives a "genuine Scotch recipe".

225g/8oz flour
80g/3oz caster sugar
pinch salt
80g/3oz margarine
1 egg
1 egg yolk
225g/8oz icing sugar
4 dsp water
50g/2oz dessicated coconut

Makes 10

Preheat oven to gas mark 6, 200°C, 400°F. Stir flour, caster sugar and salt together. Rub in the margarine and then bind to a stiff dough using the egg and egg yolk. Turn out on to a floured surface and press into a flat cake. Cut in quarters and divide each into five pieces. Roll each piece into a ball and arrange on a greased baking tray. Bake for 15 minutes, then leave to cool.

Mix together half the icing sugar and 1 dsp water to make a stiff icing and use to sandwich the cakes in pairs. Mix remaining icing sugar with 3 dsp water to make a thinner icing and dip the cakes into this before rolling in coconut and drying on bun trays.

Aberdeen Crullas

These delicate sugary plaits are mainly associated with the fine baking traditions of Aberdeen. The name probably derives from the Gaelic word *kril*, meaning a small cake or bannock. There may also be a link with the Netherlands: *krullen* means to curl, and Dutch fish curers had frequent contact with the North-east of Scotland.

225g/8oz self-raising flour
pinch salt
½ tsp ground ginger or nutmeg
50g/2oz butter
50g/2oz caster sugar
1 egg
1 tbsp buttermilk (or Greek-style yoghurt)
oil for frying
icing sugar

Makes 12

Sift flour with salt and spice. In a separate bowl, cream the butter and sugar together. Beat in the egg, adding a little flour to prevent curdling. Stir in rest of flour, adding buttermilk to make a fairly stiff dough. Roll out thinly in a 30 cm/12 inch square and cut into 12 sections approximately 10 cm by 7.5 cm/4 inch by 3 inch. Slice each lengthways into 3 strips, but leave the top uncut. Plait to form the crullas, then fold outer strips over the centre strip and pinch ends to seal. Fry in hot oil until golden. Drain on kitchen paper and dredge with icing sugar. Eat hot or cold.

BISCUITS AND TRAYBAKES

Broonie

This is a traditional oatmeal gingerbread from Orkney. In her book, *The Scots Kitchen*, Marian McNeill recalls being offered some as a child by a friend who had brought it as her school "piece". The name comes from the old Norse word *bruni*, meaning a thick bannock.

175g/6oz plain flour
pinch salt
1 tsp (level) baking powder
110g/4oz soft brown sugar
1 tsp (heaped) ground ginger
175g/6oz medium oatmeal
2 tbsp (heaped) butter
2 tbsp treacle or molasses
1 egg, beaten
275ml/10 fl oz buttermilk

Preheat oven to gas mark 4, 180°C, 350°F. Sift flour with salt, baking powder, brown sugar and ginger and stir into oatmeal. Rub in the butter. In a separate bowl melt the treacle and blend with the egg and most of the buttermilk. Add the liquid to the oatmeal mixture and stir well. Add enough buttermilk to make the mixture a dropping consistency. Turn into a greased 900g/2lb loaf tin and bake for about 1¼ hours or until well risen. Do not cut until quite cold.

Shortbread

Shortbread, particularly associated with Christmas and Hogmanay, is a relic of the Yule bannock – a round cake notched to suggest the sun's rays. Once made with oats, it was often set in a carved mould or strewn with caraway seeds or candied peel. There are many recipes and variations, but shortbread appears in prettiest guise as "petticoat tails", possibly from the French *petites gatelles*. It is claimed that Mary, Queen of Scots was very fond of them.

110g/4oz butter
50g/2oz caster sugar
110g/4oz plain flour
50g/2oz semolina or cornflour

Makes 1 round

Preheat oven to gas mark 3, 160°C, 325°F. Cream butter and then beat in sugar, followed by the sifted flour and semolina. Mix until a dough is formed then roll out into a circle or square around 18 cm/7 inch in diameter. If using a mould, press dough into shape, level with a rolling pin, then turn out onto a baking tray, patterned side up. Bake for 35-45 minutes, or until pale gold in colour. Cut into triangles or squares while still warm and dust with caster sugar.

To shape traditional petticoat tails, roll out the dough quite thinly and cut into a round, using a dinner plate. Using a tumbler, cut out a smaller circle from the centre. Cut remaining ring into eight sections and bake as above. To serve, set the small circle in the middle of a plate and arrange the petticoat "flounces" around it.

Flakemeal Crunchies

This is an updated version of the ever-popular oat biscuits. The coating of demerara sugar adds a special crunch and is an inspired touch.

175g/6oz flour
1 tsp baking soda
1 tsp baking powder
175g/6oz caster sugar
110g/4oz butter
110g/4oz white pastry fat
1 egg
110g/4oz rolled oats (flakemeal)
50g/2oz Weetabix, crushed
50g/2oz cornflakes, roughly crushed
50g/2oz coconut
80g/3oz demerara sugar

Makes 30

Preheat oven to gas mark 4, 180°C, 350°F and grease two baking trays. Sift flour, baking soda and baking powder together. Cream together caster sugar, butter and pastry fat. Add egg and mix well, then fold in flour mixture, cereals and coconut.

Shape into balls the size of a large walnut and roll each in demerara sugar. Flatten into rounds, place on baking trays and bake for 20-25 minutes until golden brown.

Currant Squares

Even in the age of convenience foods, home baking skills are flourishing, though the preference has shifted from large cakes to traybakes. Here is an unsurpassed favourite, especially when made with a delicate flaky pastry.

Flaky Pastry:
140g/5oz firm butter or margarine, grated
175g/6oz flour
pinch salt
iced water

Filling:
110g/4oz butter
80g/3oz sugar
225g/8oz currants
pinch spice
1 lemon, rind and juice
1 large apple, grated
1 slice bread, crumbled
egg yolk or milk to glaze
caster sugar

Makes 20

To make pastry: freeze butter or margarine for half an hour before grating. Sift flour and salt, then add butter or margarine and, using a palette knife, mix into flour. Add iced water until a dough is formed. Wrap and chill in fridge. Put all filling ingredients in a saucepan and bring to boiling point. Set aside to cool. Preheat oven to gas mark 6, 200°C, 400°F.

Roll out half the pastry very thinly and line a swiss roll tin. Pour on currant filling, spreading evenly, then cover with the rest of the pastry. Glaze with egg or milk and bake for 30 minutes or until light gold in colour. Dust with caster sugar and cut into squares when cool.

DESSERTS AND CHEESES

Lila's Apple Tart

This is how the best baker in my neighbourhood makes this universal family favourite. It combines the tartness of Bramleys, a couple of Cox's Pippins and, following the old books, a quince for superb flavour.

Shortcrust Pastry:
225g/8oz self raising flour
pinch salt
50g/2oz white pastry fat
50g/2oz good quality margarine
1 egg, beaten
water

Filling:
450g/1lb Bramley apples, peeled, cored and thinly sliced
225g/8oz Cox's Pippins, peeled, cored and thinly sliced
1 quince, grated (optional)
3 tbsp (heaped) sugar
nutmeg or cloves, grated
caster sugar to dust

To make the pastry: Sift the flour and salt into a large mixing bowl. Cut the pastry fat and margarine into small cubes and rub into the flour until the mixture resembles breadcrumbs. Mix the egg with a little water, reserve some to use as a glaze, and use the rest to bind the flour into a dough. Then wrap and chill in the fridge for 30 minutes.

Preheat oven to gas mark 6, 200°C, 400°F, warm a baking sheet, and grease and line a 24 cm/9 inch pie dish. Roll out a little more than half the pastry on a floured surface and line the pie dish. Place apples and quince (if using) into the dish and add sugar and a little freshly grated nutmeg or cloves.

Roll out the rest of the pastry to form a lid. Brush the rim of the pastry base with water and place the lid on top. Seal and flute edges and make a few slits in the lid to allow steam to escape. Glaze with reserved egg and sprinkle with caster sugar. Place pie dish on the warmed baking sheet and bake for 30 minutes. Serve with cream.

Country Rhubarb Cake

In the early eighteenth century, the Duke of Atholl had a famous "Turkey rhubarb" plantation at Blair Castle, from which he supplied an eminent Edinburgh druggist with rhubarb roots for grinding up as a purgative.

Scone dough:
340g/12oz plain flour
½ tsp baking soda
pinch salt
50g/2oz caster sugar
80g/3oz butter
1 egg
175ml/6 fl oz buttermilk

Filling:
700g/1½lb rhubarb, roughly chopped
200-250g/7-9oz sugar
white of 1 egg, whisked
caster sugar to dust

Preheat oven to gas mark 4, 180°C, 350°F, and grease a 25 cm/10 inch deep pie dish. Sieve flour, baking soda and salt into a mixing bowl. Add caster sugar and rub in butter. In a separate bowl, beat the egg together with the buttermilk and gradually add this to the flour until a dough is formed.

Knead lightly on a floured surface and divide dough into two. Roll out one half and use it to line the pie dish. Fill the dish with the rhubarb and sprinkle with the sugar (the quantity required depends on the tartness of the rhubarb).

Roll out the remaining dough to form a pastry lid. Brush the rim of the pastry base with water and put on the lid. Glaze with the whisked egg white and sprinkle with caster sugar. Make steam slits in the lid and bake for 50-60 minutes or until the crust is lightly browned and the fruit is soft. Serve warm with cream. This pie is also delicious if made with apples.

Clootie Dumpling

This pudding takes its name from the cloth, or clout, in which it is boiled.

175g/6oz butter
350g/12oz flour
100g/4oz sugar
1 tsp baking soda
1 tsp cinnamon
1 tsp ginger
450g/1lb sultanas
225g/8oz currants
1 tbsp syrup
1 tbsp treacle
2 eggs (beaten)
milk to mix

Rub butter into the dry ingredients. Make a well and add the syrup, treacle, beaten egg and enough milk to make a stiff mix.

Prepare the pudding cloth by dipping it into boiling water and then dusting it generously with flour. Put the mix on the cloth and tie well with string, allowing a large enough pocket for the pudding to expand. Boil for 3 hours.

Atholl Brose Pudding

Originally served as a drink, with cream this can become a rich and delicious dessert, a sort of Scottish syllabub.

300ml/½pt double cream
50g/2oz pinhead oatmeal (toasted)
3 tbsp heather honey
75ml/3 fl oz whisky

Whip cream until firm. Stir in the oatmeal with the honey. Chill then, just before serving, mix in the whisky.

Almond Flory

A favourite sweet during Edinburgh's golden age, this lovely latticed tart contains a rich Florentine almond filling, flavoured with orangeflower water and laced with brandy. Serve warm with cream and a dish of thinly sliced, ice-cold oranges to cut the richness.

1 packet frozen puff pastry

Filling:
110g/4oz ground almonds
1 tsp orangeflower water
zest of 1 lemon, grated
1 egg
1 egg yolk
80ml/3 fl oz cream
1 tbsp brandy
50g/2oz butter, softened
110g/4oz dried mixed fruit
110g/4oz soft brown sugar
pinch each cinnamon and nutmeg, freshly ground
milk to glaze

Defrost pastry and preheat oven to gas mark 7, 220°C, 425°F. Reserve enough dough for the lattice top, then roll out the pastry thinly to form a dinner plate-sized circle. Dampen a baking sheet with cold water and lay pastry circle on top. Brush around the edge with egg, then roll edges over and pinch to make a small rim. Combine the filling ingredients and spread the mixture on the pastry base. Use the reserved pastry to make a lattice top, then glaze with milk and chill in the fridge for 20 minutes.

Bake for approximately 35 minutes or until nicely golden. Remove from oven and sprinkle with sugar. This tart can also be baked in a loose-bottomed flan tin if you prefer.

Coffee with Drambuie

Drambuie is *the* liqueur of Scotland and has an ancient and honourable pedigree. Fleeing from the English forces, Bonnie Prince Charlie took refuge with the Mackinnons of Strathaird on Skye. As a gift for their hospitality, he gave them the recipe for his own liqueur. It is still made to this day from that secret recipe based, naturally, upon whisky. Coffee with Drambuie is delicious served at the end of a meal.

1 measure Drambuie
1-2 tsp soft brown sugar
pot of strong coffee
double cream

To make each serving take a stemmed glass and warm. Put in the Drambuie, stir in the brown sugar and fill with coffee to just an inch below the rim.

Stir until the sugar is fully dissolved then pour on the cream over the back of a teaspoon, so that it floats on the surface.

Scottish Cheeses

There are some delicious and distinctive Scottish cheeses of which these are my favourites.

Caboc

This cheese has been made in the Highlands for more than 400 years and is quite the most distinctive. It is a rich, creamy cheese of soft consistency shaped like a croquette and rolled in oatmeal, which gives it a very special nutty taste.

Orkney

Made in the islands to the north of the mainland from skimmed milk. It is like a mild Cheddar, and is available in red or white. The smoked ones have the best flavour.

Dunlop

Similar to Cheddar, available in red or white and is named after a village in Ayrshire. A local woman who fled to Ireland to avoid religious persecution in the late seventeenth century, Barbara Gilmour, brought the recipe back with her. Soft with a mellow flavour.

Stewart Cheeses

The Stewart cheeses are a Scottish version of Stilton. They come in blue or white and are slightly milder than Stilton. The blue cheese is generally more popular, the white being rather salty.

Crowdie

This is a very old type of cheese traditionally made in the crofts of the Highlands. It is now available commercially, usually in cartons as it is a very soft cheese. It is made with milk fresh from the cow and, unusually, is only semi-cooked. Excellent with salads and on oatcakes and bannocks.

CONFECTIONERY

Butterscotch

Those with a sweet tooth will enjoy the sweet and creamy taste of butterscotch. This recipe makes about 450g/1lb.

450g/1lb soft brown sugar
225g/½lb butter (creamed)
juice of 1 lemon

Dissolve the brown sugar in a pan. When it turns to liquid add the butter and the lemon. Allow to boil but stir gently the whole time for 15 minutes or so. The right consistency is achieved when, if a little is dropped into very cold water, it hardens.

Beat your mixture firmly for 5 minutes; pour onto a buttered tin and when it has cooled mark it into squares with a knife. When cold it will set hard. Tap the bottom of the tin with a rolling pin and it will break up into squares.

Instead of the lemon, some people prefer a ginger flavour and for this you should substitute a heaped teaspoon of ground ginger for the lemon juice.

Edinburgh Rock

Fergusons were the great Edinburgh rock makers and here is their secret, patent recipe for the sweet which has travelled the world.

450g/1lb granulated or crushed lump sugar
200ml/⅜pt water
½ tsp cream of tartar
food colouring

Heat the sugar and water until the sugar is dissolved. When about to boil add the cream of tartar and boil without stirring until it reaches 130°C, 250°F, or until it forms a hard ball in cold water.

Take from the heat and add colouring as required. Remember the colour will fade as the candy is 'pulled'. Pour on to a buttered marble slab, or into buttered candy bars. Cool slightly and turn the edges to the centre with an oiled scraper, but do not stir.

When cool enough to handle, dust it with icing sugar, and 'pull' it evenly and quickly, taking care not to twist it, until it becomes opaque and dull. This should be done in a warm kitchen, or near a heater if the candy becomes stiff too quickly. Draw out the candy into strips and cut into short lengths with a pair of oiled scissors.

Leave in a warm room on greased paper for at least 24 hours, when the rock will become powdery and soft. It can be stored in an air-tight tin. If the candy remains sticky, it means that it has not been pulled enough.

Further Reading

Ena Baxter, *Ena Baxter's Scottish Cookbook*, Stirling, 1974.
Catherine Brown, *Scottish Regional Recipes*, Glasgow, 1981.
Theodora Fitzgibbon, *A Taste of Scotland*, London, 1970.
The Lady Glentruim, *Dinners in a Scottish Castle*, Edinburgh, 1983.
F. Marian McNeill, *The Book of Breakfasts*, Edinburgh, 1975.
F. Marian McNeill, *Recipes from Scotland*, Edinburgh, 1946.
F. Marian McNeill, *The Scots Kitchen*, Glasgow, 1925.
Janet Murray, *With A Fine Feeling for Food*, Aberdeen, 1972.
Queen's College, Glasgow, *The Glasgow Cookery Book*, Glasgow, 1975.
Janet Warren, *A Feast of Scotland*, London, 1979.
Molly Weir, *Molly Weir's Recipes*, Edinburgh, 1980.

Acknowledgements

Page 6   © istockphoto.com/creacart

Page 14   © istockphoto.com/Difydave

Page 22   © istockphoto.com/swalls

Page 28   © fabfoodpix.com

Page 36   © fabfoodpix.com

Page 44   © istockphoto.com/PaulCowan

Page 54   © istockphoto.com/creacart

Page 70   © John Murphy

Page 76   © istockphoto.com/alyssum

Page 88   © John Murphy

Index